How to Bec

The Beginner's G
Actor and Gett...

Copyright © 2016 by Melissa Kennedy

All rights reserved.

This book or any portion thereof may not be reproduced or used in any manner whatsoever without the express written permission of the publisher except for the use of brief quotations in a book review.

Contents

Introduction 5

  Why This Book? 6

Chapter 1 – Seven Things You Need to Know 8

  Acting is a Business.....................................8

  Know Your Type...9

  The First Year is the Toughest 10

  Competition is Cut-Throat 11

  Looks Matter (to a Degree) 12

  Know Your Limitations...............................12

  Rejection is the Norm 13

Chapter 2 – Laying the Groundwork 14

  Headshots...14

  Resume 15

  Networking 16

  Keep Your Skills Honed 18

  Have a Safety Net 19

Chapter 3 – Do You Need an Agent / Manager? 20

  Pros of Having an Agent 20

  Cons of Having an Agent.............................21

  What's the Difference Between an Agent and a
  Manager?..22

How to Find an Agent 23

Chapter 4 – The Art of Auditioning 25

Read the Audition Notice 25

Make Your First Fifteen Seconds' Count 26

Put Up a False Front 26

Appearance Counts 27

What *Not* to Do at an Audition.................................29

What Casting Directors Are Looking For 30

How to Find Auditions and Open Casting Calls 32

Chapter 5 – Handling Rejection......................................33

It's Not Personal 33

It Could be Personal 34

Your Special Vibe 35

Should You "Embrace" Rejection? 35

Tips to Minimize Disappointment 36

Focus on the Positive...36

Be Honest with Yourself 37

Have Somewhere to Be and People to Be With.........37

Chapter 6 - Additional Tips and Trivia 40

Conclusion 44

4

Introduction

This book is not for the fainthearted, so be prepared. I'm going to give you the cold hard facts and I will pull no punches. If you're serious about becoming an actor and breaking into movies, empty platitudes and pep talks about staying positive, believing in yourself and never giving up are not going to get you anywhere. Your mother can give you encouragement. I'm going to give you tools and techniques that will help you market yourself as an actor and put you on the road to getting your first role.

Having said that, I commend you on your courage and resolve. It is a very unique and determined person who decides to become an actor. Being an actor requires a variety of often contradictory traits. I would say you need to be mildly schizophrenic. You are no doubt sensitive, passionate and vulnerable. You have the ability to go deep into yourself to summon up profound emotions. Yet you need the hide of a rhinoceros to avoid being crippled by rejection. You have to be egotistical but humble. You need to stay true to yourself but know when to compromise, in order to pay the bills. You are a romantic yet sometimes you need to be ruthless in a fiercely competitive business.

But if you believe you have a real talent to share with the world, with patience, perseverance and a well-laid out plan, there's no reason why you can't achieve success as a screen actor and hopefully, even stardom.

Why This Book?

Many aspiring actors simply don't know where to start. They have some vague idea that all they have to do is take a couple of acting classes, run around to casting calls and auditions and sooner or later they're bound to get hired. The harsh fact is that there are millions of super talented actors who never get a break, simply because they don't know how to put themselves out there. They don't have a method or concrete plan of action.

Another group of would-be actors are those who embrace the 'struggling artist' notion. All they have to do is move to Hollywood, work at McDonalds and keep the faith because sooner or later, they'll be discovered by some hot-shot producer. I'm not ruling out the possibility; sheer luck can be a factor in almost any career - but seriously, how likely is it? We know that the majority of big-screen stars spent years honing their skills and facing rejection until they got their big breaks. Many started out in commercials, or as walk-ons and extras. Some were told that they just didn't have what it takes (more about that in chapter 5).

Staking your future on random hopes and fantasies will only lead to disillusionment and will likely cause you to give up. Having a plan in place will make your job a little easier and help prepare you for what to expect. The tools and techniques provided here will help you stay on track by keeping you focused on your goal, even if your big break takes some time. Let's start with some basic things you need to know if you want to become an actor.

Chapter 1 – Seven Things You Need to Know

The following points are they key basics any actor needs to know. These seven basic rules are simple but crucial because they will get you off on the right foot. Consider them broad guidelines that will help you better navigate the ups and downs of your career path and avoid unnecessary setbacks.

Acting is a Business

If you were setting up a business, would you rent office space, hire a secretary, then sit at your desk and wait for things to happen? Well, maybe – if you wanted to go bankrupt within a week. Acting is the same. It's a business, and if you want to succeed, don't expect your talent alone to carry you through. Like any business, you need to know the ropes; the supply and demand of your market, specific "needs" you can provide, peak seasons, how to stay ahead of the competition and how to keep abreast of the numbers and statistics

For example, knowing that about 95% of all registered professional actors are out of work at any given time is an important statistic to know, to realistically assess your chances and whether you want acting to be a second job or career.

Wages are another important factor to consider. Screen and television actors are generally well-paid but wages may differ depending on experience and the work itself.

Consider what you are going to invest in your acting career. Will you take a year off work or school in order to solely pursue acting? Will you hire an agent or a manager? Will you take certain classes or hire an acting coach?

In addition, having your thumb on the pulse of things and being knowledgeable of the business side of acting will lend you more credibility and professionalism as an actor.

Know Your Type

Type can be a crucial factor of success early on in your career. You're more likely to get hired for roles that suit your type, and having that experience on your resume will allow you to branch out and diversify later on. Of course, a good actor needs to be versatile to a certain degree, but every actor does have a type that they are strongest at. **Remember, acting is a business and your type is your** "brand." That is what you need to market, first and foremost.

For example, if you are the boy / girl next-door type, that's what you need to focus on in the beginning, then you will be more likely to get that first job. More specifically, knowing what type you're *not* should be an indicator of what roles you might not want to audition for. It will save you a lot of frustration and rejection in the long run.

Take this short quiz to identify what type of actor you are:

http://www.proprofs.com/quiz-school/story.php?title=acting-advice-what-type-are-you

The First Year is the Toughest

This is one fact you really need to hammer home to yourself. You're probably not going to get much work - if any - during your first year. In fact, it may take longer than a year. Being prepared for a long struggle is vital. There are so many actors who give up too soon, simply because they didn't realize it would be so hard. You will need every ounce of dedication, passion and resolve to carry you through. This is the time to surround yourself with supportive and encouraging people who believe in you. Take advantage of this period to hone your skills, take voice or dance lessons and stay up to date, by attending lectures or networking with other actors.

Now of course, this rule is not carved in stone. You might get your first role in a couple of months, or even on your very first audition. If you do, that's great! You're one of the rare lucky ones. But being prepared for a very tough first year will help you avoid getting disillusioned.

Competition is Cut-Throat

Competition in any profession is a given; but in the acting business, competition is fierce, fierce, fierce, simply because there are too few roles and too much talent. You will see this for yourself when you walk into an audition and find hundreds of actors vying for the same role.

The chapter on how to prepare and behave at auditions, plus the other techniques in this book will give you the edge you need to stand out in the crowd and market yourself to your best advantage. Constant competition is simply a way of life in the movie industry. Even megastars compete for juicy roles or to work with a certain director.

Looks Matter (to a Degree)

Unless you're playing a masked chainsaw-wielding maniac or a Chewbacca type character, looks do matter to a certain degree. Be honest with yourself; look in the mirror and assess where you stand in the looks department.

You don't have to be spectacularly good-looking to be a successful screen actor. Mike Myers, Danny DeVito and Jim Carrey are not your typical heartthrobs but they are huge megastars in their own right. What I mean to say is that you will want to keep in mind that your looks may be perfect for certain roles but not for others. You may have a certain quirk in your features, a special type of grin or facial expression that would be perfect for a comedy role or a villain's role. You may not have the physique to play an action role. Again, this is not carved in stone. Casting directors have their own perspectives sometimes but it's always good to be realistic.

Know Your Limitations

If you weren't born with comic talent, you will never be a big comedy actor. If you just don't have a good voice, you will never play a starring role in a musical, no matter how many lessons you take. It's better to focus on your strengths to land your first role. Learning to be the best actor that you can be means acknowledging your limitations and celebrating your strengths.

Rejection is the Norm

This is without a doubt the toughest part of being an actor. Rejection hurts, especially for an actor struggling to get that first role. Just know that it is the rule rather than the exception in the acting business. Out of the dozens auditioning for that single role, only one person will get it and all the others hopefuls will be rejected. The next time around, that same person may be rejected while another gets the role. In chapter four, you will learn how to handle and accept rejection. And yes, it does get easier over time.

With these basic rules under your belt, you are now ready to start laying the groundwork for becoming a full-fledged actor and landing your first role.

Chapter 2 – Laying the Groundwork

Since acting is a business and any business requires planning and investment, the following steps are the major investments you need to make to build your career as an actor:

Headshots

A killer headshot is your most important marketing tool. It should make you come across as a pro. It should make you come across as unique. Your headshot should make a casting director say *"That's just the face I'm looking for"* Here's what you need to do:

Go to a Pro

More specifically, a professional photographer who specializes in headshots. He will know the best angle to shoot you from, he will know about the right backgrounds and lighting to use and he will know how to bring out the best in your features. Whatever you do, do not attempt to take a home-made headshot, as in having your brother take a close-up of you in the back yard or in the scenic outdoors. Casting directors will not see this as unique or quirky. You will only succeed in coming across as very unprofessional.

Don't Skimp

A good headshot will cost from $400 to $1200. Anything less will not get you the desired quality. Be prepared to pay another $100 to get your headshots professionally duplicated. I cannot emphasize enough that this is one thing you don't want to be cheap with.

Go for Personality

A good headshot should simply look like you on a good hair day. Don't go overboard with makeup, fancy hairstyle or weird glasses or hats. The traditional "glamour" photo is out and weird headgear is just that – weird. Just be yourself, and let your natural personality shine through. If you're a naturally serious person, a big grin will come across as strained and artificial. If you have a bubbly personality, a serious expression will come across as fake. **Remember, casting directors will expect you to look like your headshot when you go in for an audition.**

Resume

You resume will always be sent in together with your headshot and is equally important in letting casting directors know just who you are.

An acting resume differs from a regular resume in that it includes your physical details (height, weight, and hair and eye color). It should also contain your work history (in your case, assuming that you have no work history, you can simply write "None yet." Make sure to list any professional training you may have had and any special skills such as singing, dancing, impersonating accents, or any athletic skills such as martial arts, boxing, etc.

Here is a free template you can download to help you create a great resume:

http://www.doctemplates.net/acting-resume-template-build-your-own-resume-now/

Networking

Networking is the new buzzword among career professionals who are now beginning to realize its importance. Having a solid network of professionals from within the film industry is key to building your career.

There are bound to be networking events or meetups for actors in your area. Find out where and when they are and make sure you attend as many as possible, as frequently as possible.

Why is Networking Important?

- It's your best tool for marketing yourself as a budding actor.

- Networking events and meetups will keep you in the hub of things and ensure you stay current with what's going on.

- The more connections you make, the better your chances will be of getting a role through one of them or of being introduced to important people.

Important Tips

- Never huddle alone in a corner with a drink. You might as well have stayed home. Circulate, circulate, circulate. Try to meet and talk to at least five new people at every event you attend.

- Always have copies of your resume and headshots with you. You never know!

Online groups fall under this heading. Although this is not technically networking, a lot can be said for joining an online group or forum. There are literally hundreds to choose from and they cover a huge range of preferences and specializations. Online groups are an excellent way to connect with like-minded people, to make friends, share experiences and advice and to air grievances. They're also a great place to find support and encouragement when you've had one too many rejections!

Keep Your Skills Honed

Stay busy between auditions by working on your skills and adding new ones to your repertoire. A good artist knows that acting is a continuous learning process; there's always something new to learn or something to improve on.

Take dancing or singing lessons; take voice lessons, join a local theater group, get together with friends to read plays or scripts aloud, or take a class relevant to your acting interests. Even though you may not be working yet, these activities will keep you motivated. They will also make great additions to your resume.

Have a Safety Net

Don't throw everything to the wind and just rush off to 'be an actor'. Without the security of something to fall back on, you won't be able to really focus on your acting career.

Unless you're indecently wealthy, you need to assess your financial situation and plan for survival during the very lean first years. This may mean finding a job that that will pay the bills until you get your break. You may have a partner who is willing to support the both of you while you concentrate on your career, or super supportive parents who'll send you a monthly check. Whatever it may be, just make sure you have that kind of security in place. **Never depend on your savings to carry you through.** Even a part-time job is a much better option.

Chapter 3 – Do You Need an Agent / Manager?

There's no clear consensus on whether having an agent early in your career is the better option. Some people will tell you that an agent is vital to jump-start your career and give you credibility as a serious actor. Other people will warn you that an agent can harm an actor by pressuring him to accept any role that comes along, without really focusing on building his career. Many actors have told me that it doesn't matter whether you have an agent or not; you can make it either way.

In this chapter, I'm going to lay out the pros and cons and leave the choice to you. My personal view is that to have or not to have an agent is not a key factor of success. Many successful actors have broken into movies on their own. However, I will lay out the facts for you and leave the decision to you.

Pros of Having an Agent

• Agents have connections. They can get you introduced to important people in the industry, set up meetings with producers and casting directors and maybe even get you invited to important events.

- Agents have an insider's view of the business. They often know of upcoming roles or auditions before they are announced and can help you get your foot in the door early on.

- They help you settle disputes that may arise.

- They know the going rates and can negotiate your contract better than you can.

- A good agent will give you advice on headshots and how to audition.

- An agent's insider knowledge will allow him to send your resume to casting directors looking for your specific type.

- An actor with an agent is sometimes seen as having more credibility.

Cons of Having an Agent

- The 10% fee! Many actors just don't want to pay an agent's fee (which may be quite substantial if the job is a big one).

- An agent's job is to get you a job. He also wants his 10%, so he may not be as selective as you would like, with regard to the roles he finds you. You may find yourself getting small roles regularly but not really going anywhere with your career.

• It's a common myth that having an agent will get you jobs faster than you can on your own. Not true. It may take an agent months or even longer to get you a job.

• Another common myth is that an agent will get you big, juicy roles early on in your career. Not true. An agent will get you anything he can.

What's the Difference Between an Agent and a Manager?

Surprisingly, many actors don't know the difference and think that an agent and a manager are the same thing. Agents are different than managers in the level of personalized service each provides you with.

An agent is concerned with only one thing – getting you your next job. Except in rare cases, the relationship between you and your agent will be highly impersonal. A manager on the other hand will have a much more personal relationship with you. A manager will make you and your career as a whole, his focus and will be much more involved in your life. He will guide you in every aspect of your career development, perhaps even advising you against certain roles, which an agent may not do.

A manager may even give you advice on your appearance or other aspects that may be an obstacle to you getting roles.

It may not be practical to hire a manager early on in your career. Managers typically get 20% of your earnings, which is really quite a lot when you're only getting a few small jobs early on. Realistically, it's better to get a manager when you have a real career to manage.

How to Find an Agent

The best way is to contact SAG (Screen Actors Guild) or AFTRA (American Federation of Television and Radio Actors), requesting an agent in your area. The list will specify each type of agent (theatrical, screen, kids only, etc). Choose several agencies that you feel are the best for you and CALL FIRST to enquire if they are accepting new clients. If so, send them your headshots, resume and a short cover letter asking them to represent you. If you send these by email, make sure your headshot is cleanly scanned, sharp and clear. I personally recommend mailing in your resume and headshots. It's more professional, and an email easily goes unnoticed in a busy talent agency.

Keep a record of which agencies you've contacted so that you don't mail out to them again. Within a week, you should start receiving replies. It's then your job to shortlist the agencies that you feel will best represent you, then narrow that down to one.

Having an agent or a manager is entirely up to you. Not having one will not hinder you from breaking into movies, nor will having one guarantee success. Searching for an agent should not be a priority at the start of your career but if you feel this will benefit you, by all means, go ahead. If you would prefer to go the first year entirely on your own, that's perfectly fine too. The essential point is: It's ultimately your talent that will land you that first job.

NEVER pay an agent or manager anything upfront. If an agency or company asks for an "agency fee", know that this is a scam. The only time you pay an agent or manager is when he has gotten you a job and you have actually been paid it.

Chapter 4 – The Art of Auditioning

This is really what it all boils down to. No amount of agents, contacts or lessons are going to compensate for your natural and unique talent on the audition stage. It's a killer audition that will make casting directors sit up and take notice. That's why auditioning is an art that you need to perfect. You can be amazingly talented, perfect for the role and yet be rejected because you simply did not present yourself well, or failed to get across that certain vibe a casting director looks for. The following does and don'ts discussed here are no guarantee that you will breeze through every audition every time and get the part. However, I can promise that they will give you a flying head start and help you come across as a serious and dedicated professional. Here are the basics:

Read the Audition Notice

Some auditions will give a brief description. It will tell you if the role requires you to present a monologue of your own choosing. Some auditions are based on "cold reads", where you will walk in and be given a script to read from, without the chance to prepare beforehand. Read the notice carefully so that you understand exactly what is required and prepare accordingly. In addition, make sure you are suitable for the role. If the notice says "Tall, thin man in his fifties", don't waste your time if you're on the short side and in your twenties.

Make Your First Fifteen Seconds' Count

The first impression you make on the casting panel is crucial and will affect how they will perceive your reading. Acting coaches recommend the three C's formula to make a great first impression: Comfortable, Confident, Charismatic. I recommend that you practice walking into an audition and greeting the panel. Practice before a mirror or in front of your friends and have them give you honest feedback. Make sure that your head is high, shoulders straight and that your step is firm and self-assured. Nervousness usually causes people to slouch or hunch their shoulders, so practice to make sure that you don't so this!

Put Up a False Front

No actor on the planet feels totally confident walking into an audition. I promise you that if De Niro had to go in for an audition tomorrow, he'd be nervous as hell. The key is not to show it. You need to walk in with a firm step, confident smile and an air of calm self-assurance. Casting directors have no sympathy for shy, bumbling actors. This includes replying to their questions in monosyllables.

Speak naturally and clearly, letting your personality shine through.

How can you be confident when you're shaking in your shoes? You're an actor, right? Play the part! Seriously; pretend you're some super cool, suave, James Bond type character – just don't overdo it. And don't despair; the more you audition and get the hang of it, the more you will be able to walk in with confidence.

Appearance Counts

Walking into an audition wearing flip-flops, grubby jeans or a wrinkled t-shirt will not scream 'artistic' to the casting panel; it will scream 'sloppy'. On the other extreme, auditioning in a suit and tie will probably creep out the casting director. Simplicity and good grooming is the key.

Giving the casting panel the courtesy of looking presentable and well turned-out will speak volumes to them about you as an actor, who is professional and serious about his career, as well as respectful of them.

A clean, pressed shirt and jeans or a simple dress are perfect for auditioning in. Clean, casual and not too dressy is the first step in impressing the casting panel. It also allows them to focus on your acting, not on the weird hat you're wearing.

Whatever you do, do not go in dressed for the part. This is in no way original, unique or impressive. If you're auditioning for a bellboy's role, please wear your normal clothes and not a bellboy's uniform. Enough said.

Practice in the clothes you're going to wear. Make sure you can sit down and stand up and move around freely and that nothing feels too tight or uncomfortable.

Always remember to bring copies of your resume and headshots, as you may be asked to leave them behind for a call-back.

Don't bring props. Just read the scene clearly and enunciate every word. Don't use weird accents unless the role specifically calls for it and don't distract the casting panel by moving around too much, unless it is necessary.

Be polite. Greet the panel politely and address them as "*Sir*" or "*Ma'am*". Reply to any questions graciously and wish them a nice day as you're leaving. This may sound silly but it does score you points. Casting directors are not just looking for talent but also for actors who are courteous, accommodating and can get along well with others.

What *Not* to Do at an Audition

• Don't be cocky. There's a fine line between confident and cocky – never overstep it. Greeting the casting panel with *"Hiya guys, what's up?"* is ungracious and cocky. *"Good morning, thank you for seeing me"* is pleasant and confident. Cocky is never the way to make a good first impression.

• Never touch the casting director's belongings and never touch the casting director. Imagine how you would feel if a stranger did that to you? It's creepy, to say the least. **Remember, your behavior at the audition is an indication of how you will behave on a film set.**

• Never look directly at the casting director during your scene to gauge his or her response to your acting. It makes them feel uncomfortable and makes you lose your focus.

• Smoking or chewing gum at an audition will immediately get you off on the wrong foot.

• Don't make excuses. Casting directors don't want to hear that you have a bad cold or that you've had a long day at work. If you feel you did badly, that's your problem. Thank the panel for their time and leave.

● Never argue. If you are told that you're not the person they're looking for, don't argue back or try to convince the panel that they're wrong.

● Never be sarcastic or rude. Being respectful and charming will increase your chances for a callback.

What Casting Directors Are Looking For

The casting director is not some kind of glorified talent show judge. He is a highly specialized and respected professional in the film world. Directors depend on a casting director's experience and discerning eye to choose actors that fit the respective roles to make a great movie come together. In other words, the casting director has a bigger picture in mind when he is auditioning you. Sometimes casting can make or break a movie and this is why the casting process is vital.

Understanding the casting director's responsibility will help you make your audition more successful and even understand why you were rejected.

So, what is a casting director looking for?

A casting director wants you to wow him. Did you know that the audition process is as stressful for the casting director as it is for the actors? Think about it; the casting director's job is to find the prefect actor for the part as quickly as possible. He's actually hoping that the next actor to walk in will be the one who'll make him think, "*That's the guy I want! This part was written for him!*" In other words, your success at an audition means success for the casting director.

He wants you to have character. Casting directors want you to be direct, honest and no-nonsense. They don't have the time or patience to soothe nervous wrecks or wait on actors who have to keep starting over. They want you to answer questions articulately but concisely. Walk in, give a short greeting, read the part as best you can, thank the panel and leave.

He wants you to make bold choices. If you are asked to come in with your own prepared piece, beware of the same old bland, predictable monologues that actors tend to choose because they think it's safer. Shakespeare is great but it will not grab attention. Be daring and bold in your choice, by reading a monologue from a little-known play or movie. It will make the casting director sit up straighter and take notice.

He wants someone made for the part: If you are not what the casting director envisions, he may not change his mind, no matter how good you are. That's why you need to read audition notices carefully to make sure the part suits you, to increase your chances of success.

How to Find Auditions and Open Casting Calls

● The easiest way is to Google "*Auditions and casting calls in...*" and add your city.

● Check your local papers

● ActorsAccess.com is an excellent resource you can check out, not only to find auditions but for lots of helpful tips and information.

● Contact your local SAG-AFRA office or check out their websites. They usually post audition notices that you may not find anywhere else.

Finally, **audition much as you can.** The more practice you have, the better you will get at perfecting the art of auditioning.

Chapter 5 – Handling Rejection

Rejection is a way of life for actors, more so for actors who are just learning the ropes and are more idealistic and vulnerable. Moreover, landing that first role is no guarantee that you have broken the curse. You may still be rejected dozens of times over before you get your second and third role, and so on.

Rejection – and lots of it – is just something you must be prepared to face. It will never become totally painless but it does get easier over time.

The danger lies in letting rejection cripple you to the point where you walk into auditions prepared to fail! If you ever find yourself feeling that way it may be time give up your dream. This chapter will show you how to avoid that by putting rejection into perspective and realizing that there are many factors involved – the least of which is you personally. So, why were you rejected?

It's Not Personal

You've walked into the audition well prepared; you've laid everything on the line. You made yourself very vulnerable in front of a panel of strangers; you did everything you were supposed to do, and all you got was a curt "*Thank you – next!*" Of course, the rejection feels very personal and it hurts.

The reality is, it has nothing to do with you personally. The casting director is not your sworn enemy. In fact, he wants you to succeed because his or own reputation is on the line. He wants to cast the part as fast as he can.

As I explained before, casting directors make a living by putting a great cast together. To be brutally honest, in many cases it has nothing to do with your talent but with the image casting directors, producers or directors have of the ideal person for the role. It could be about your height, voice, weight, or some other specific feature. In other words, sometimes it's not whether you were good or bad! It's not fair but it's the truth. Keeping that thought in mind will help lessen the pain of being rejected.

It Could be Personal

Usually, this is not the case but it could be that you did something to creep out the casting directors in a major way - like arguing at length, asking to be given another chance, behaving in a menacing way, asking him / her out on a date... These are things that will get you rejected on a personal basis, which means you need to reassess and improve your behavior for future additions.

Your Special Vibe

The casting process involves hiring a whole cast of actors for a movie and not just the role you are auditioning for. The movie involves group scenes and a lot of interaction between cast members, the director and the producers. In addition to your talent, casting directors often have a feel for certain "vibes", such as a strong work ethic, your ability to get along with others, your flexibility and a willingness to follow instructions. If you come across as anti-social, overly cynical, sarcastic or downright rude, that will be an indicator of how you will behave with colleagues and bosses.

Should You "Embrace" Rejection?

Some "experts" advise actors to learn how to embrace rejection and celebrate it as a normal part of our emotional evolution. What does that even mean? Can you picture yourself skipping out of a failed audition telling yourself, *"Hurray, I got rejected! I love being rejected! I celebrate and embrace my rejection!"* I don't know about you but that sounds like a load of horse crap to me.

Nobody in his right mind can learn to love rejection and I recommend that you not waste your time reading senseless blogs / books / articles along those lines.

More realistically, rejection can make you angry, motivating you to analyze your performance, learn new skills or improve existing ones and push you to perfect your auditioning skills. Rejection can strengthen your persistence and resolve but believe me, you will never learn to love it.

Tips to Minimize Disappointment

There are several ways you can train yourself to make the disappointment a little easier to bear. Not all of them will work for every audition rejection except the last one which I highly recommend that you arrange before every audition – having somewhere to be and people to be with.

Focus on the Positive

As I mentioned before, you might give an exceptionally good performance and still be rejected because the casting director was after a certain "look." Go through the audition in your head and note all the positive aspects such as, "*I was especially confident today. I gave a killer performance. I looked great. I got some good feedback from the casting panel. I accepted the rejection graciously...*" In other words, you were super and could not have done better. Congratulate yourself on a job well done.

Focusing on the positive will lift your spirits and keep your confidence up for the next audition.

Be Honest with Yourself

Every actor instinctively knows when his performance was not up to par and no actor is brilliant every single time. If it was not one of your best auditions, be straight with yourself, pledge to do better next time and get over it. Remember, taking responsibility is one thing but beating yourself up about it is another. Do not fall victim to mental self-talk that tells you that you're a loser, a failure, that you're stupid to think you'll ever make it, etc. Simply acknowledge that you were not in your best form and move on.

Have Somewhere to Be and People to Be With

Arrange to have coffee with friends, dinner with your parents or to go to a movie with your partner. The worst thing you can do is go off somewhere by yourself to mope. It goes without saying that these get-togethers should be with people who are supportive and encouraging. This technique is without a doubt the best way to boost your confidence and self-esteem at a time when you need it most.

Let's end this chapter on a lighter note, with examples of famous stars who faced rejection at the beginning of their careers – but whom definitely had the last laugh!

Did you know that Jerry Seinfeld was fired after his very first performance (a minor role in television sitcom)? To make matters worse, someone forgot to inform him of the fact. He walked onto the set the next day to find that he'd been replaced with another actor – that is rejection on a major level.

Hollywood legend and sex goddess Marilyn Monroe was told at an audition that she'd be better off working as a secretary because she wasn't talented enough to be an actress.

Now, Stephen King is not technically an actor unless you count a couple of cameos but his rejection was so spectacular that I feel it deserves special mention. His best-selling book Carrie was rejected a whopping 30 times before it was published and later became a blockbuster movie.

Before her big break on the comedy sitcom 'I Love Lucy', Lucille Ball was considered a failure as an actress. Her own drama teachers begged her to give up and find another career.

What is the lesson to be learned from these who later became huge stars? **Never let rejection bring you down!**

Chapter 6 - Additional Tips and Trivia

This chapter is a random jumble of facts, quotes, trivia and tips that you will find informative, inspiring and amusing. The film trivia especially is a great icebreaker for networking events.

Getting your big break as an actor can sometimes be a case of sheer luck. Harrison Ford, Charlize Theron and Pamela Anderson were all "discovered" while going about their normal lives. Sarah Michelle Geller was also discovered – at the age of three, at a restaurant with her parents!

If you are a total beginner, never jump straight into auditioning no matter how good you think you are. Take an acting class or two and learn the ropes first or you will feel completely out of your depth.

"Without wonder and insight, acting is just a business. With it, it becomes creation."

~ Bette Davis

Bruce Willis, Brad Pitt, Megan Fox, Renee Zelleweger and Matt Damon started their careers as extras, and look where they are now! That's dedication and perseverance! I recommend that you try finding work as an extra until you can get a proper role. It's an invaluable experience that will allow you to get your foot in the door, teach you how movies are made and bring you into contact with a lot of industry people.

Morgan Freeman, Ben Affleck and Meg Ryan started their careers commercials. I recommend that if you get the chance to act in a commercial, grab it. Any experience you can gain early on in your career will serve you well.

Harvey Kietel is now the manager of the Actors Studio. Amazingly, he had previously auditioned there and was rejected eight years in a row!

"Real acting is impossible to spot. Do you ever catch talents like Robert Duvall or Kathy Bates acting? No. I defy you to show me where."

~ William Esper

Think of acting as a freelance job when you are first starting out. Jobs will be few and far between and this may go on for several years.

Given the fierce competition over film roles, you'd think that every other person was trying to break into movies, but the statistics say otherwise. In the United States, the number of fulltime and part-time actors is around 70,000, a very small fraction of the total workforce.

Learn how to slate. Slating is the process of stating your full name and the agency that represents you (if any) at an audition. Slating is basically giving the casting director this information clearly and concisely when he asks you to introduce yourself. The catch is that you have to slate in the character you're auditioning for. If it's a character in a commercial, your slate should be cheerful, upbeat and enthusiastic. If you're auditioning for a villain's role, your slate might be more monotone and slow, and so on. Slating is not mandatory for auditions but knowing how to do it will tell the casting director that you are a professional.

Sean Connery turned down the part of Gandalf in Lord of the Rings because he had reservations about the script. Burt Reynolds turned down the role of Indiana Jones and

John Travolta turned down the role of Forrest Gump for the same reason.

Robert Downey Jr. is Hollywood's highest earning actor at $75 million.

"I love acting. It is so much more real than life."

~ Oscar Wilde

Meryl Streep tops the list of actors with the most Oscar nominations, with 19 well-deserved nominations in total.

The biggest number of movies produced annually is not in Hollywood but in Bollywood, India, which has one of the most thriving movie industries in the world.

Get creative and find new ways to showcase your talent. Why not perform several short unique scenes with friends and upload them to YouTube? YouTube videos have a strange way of going insanely viral, making instant celebrities. You could also create a website of your own, with videos of you performing, along with "reviews" from friends and visitors include the link on your resume.

Conclusion

Acting is about pursuing your dream and making it come true. In the end, it's not only about honing your skills, preparing for auditions, getting an agent or networking. All of that is meaningless unless you can actually get jobs that will allow you to earn a living and more importantly, share your talent with an audience. Pursue your dream using the techniques provided in this book, in order to achieve your main goal, getting a role in a movie.

It's fair to ask how long you should continue to pursue your dream if you're not getting anywhere. There are thousands of actors who give up after a year or two, preferring the security of a regular paying job. Equally, there are thousands who have been in the profession for decades who have not made it big. They prefer the occasional small part or TV commercial because **they just can't imagine doing anything else. Acting is their life blood.**

Ultimately, how long you should continue to pursue your dream is totally up to you.

My own advice to you is to keep at it for as long as you possibly can. Never let a day go by that you don't work at your career. Even if you have another job, or if you have family commitments, do something for your acting career every day, even if it's just reading a short scene with your partner or friend over a glass of wine... Stay fit and healthy, continue to expand your knowledge, audition regularly and stay current by watching the latest movies and TV shows.

Sure, acting is a tough, ruthless business and making it as a film actor is an uphill battle all the way. But if you believe in yourself, work at it every day and don't drop off like so many other do, you will make it.

Finally, it has not my intention to dampen your enthusiasm or complicate things for you. I'm a big believer in following dreams. Think of where we would be today if Thomas Edison, Benjamin Franklin or Henry Ford did not have the courage and resolve to pursue their visions despite the odds. My goal was to lay out the bare facts that you will need, rather than empty "believe in yourself" pep talks.

Because ultimately, you do believe in yourself and in your ability to become a successful actor.

Best of luck!

Printed in Great Britain
by Amazon